EVA
PERÓN

FIRST LADY OF ARGENTINA

SPECIAL LIVES IN HISTORY THAT BECOME

Signature LIVES

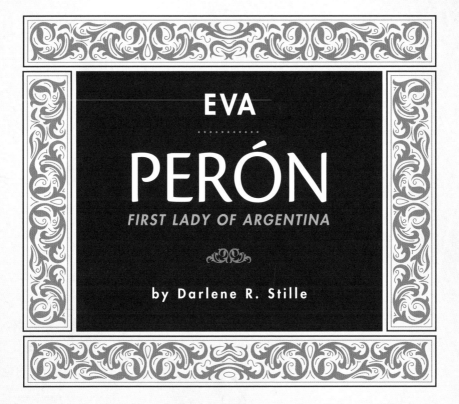

EVA

PERÓN

FIRST LADY OF ARGENTINA

by Darlene R. Stille

Content Adviser: Daniel K. Lewis, Ph.D.,
Department of History,
California State Polytechnic University

Reading Adviser: Rosemary G. Palmer, Ph.D.,
Department of Literacy, College of Education,
Boise State University

COMPASS POINT BOOKS ✦ MINNEAPOLIS, MINNESOTA

Compass Point Books
3109 West 50th Street, #115
Minneapolis, MN 55410

Visit Compass Point Books on the Internet at *www.compasspointbooks.com*
or e-mail your request to *custserv@compasspointbooks.com*

Editor: Julie Gassman
Page Production: Noumenon Creative
Photo Researcher: Marcie C. Spence
Cartographer: XNR Productions, Inc.
Library Consultant: Kathleen Baxter

Art Director: Jaime Martens
Creative Director: Keith Griffin
Editorial Director: Carol Jones
Managing Editor: Catherine Neitge

JB
PER

Library of Congress Cataloging-in-Publication Data
Stille, Darlene R.
  Eva Peron, First Lady of Argentina / by Darlene R. Stille.
     p. cm.—(Signature lives)
  Includes bibliographical references and index.
  ISBN 0-7565-1585-8 (hard cover)
  1. Perón, Eva, 1919-1952—Juvenile literature. 2. Argentina—History—
1943-1955—Juvenile literature. 3. Presidents' spouses—Argentina—
Biography—Juvenile literature. 4. Politicians—Argentina—Biography—
Juvenile literature. I. Title: First Lady of Argentina. II. Title. III. Series.
  F2849.P37S85 2006
  982.06'2092—dc22   2005025097

MODERN WORLD

From 1900 to the present day, humanity and the world have undergone major changes. New political ideas resulted in worldwide wars. Fascism and communism divided some countries, and democracy brought others together. Drastic shifts in theories and practice tested the standards of personal freedoms and religious conventions as well as science, technology, and industry. These changes have created a need for world policies and an understanding of international relations. The new mind-set of the modern world includes a focus on humanitarianism and the belief that a global economy has made the world a more connected place.

Eva Perón

1 A WOMAN OF MYTHS

ଏଚ୍ଚର୍ବ

Eva Perón stood before a crowd of 2 million cheering, chanting supporters. They jammed a broad avenue in Buenos Aires, Argentina. Some had camped out all night just to get close to her. They wanted her to run for vice president of Argentina. Her husband, Juan Perón, had been Argentina's president since 1946.

It was now August 22, 1951. Two 60-foot-high (18.3-meter-high) pictures of Juan and Eva Perón towered behind Eva, as she stood on a raised platform. The crowd chanted, "Evita, Evita," over and over again. They called her Evita, which means "little Eva," because they adored her. Since her husband had become president, Evita had done much to help poor Argentines, and now they wanted her to rule alongside him. She held up her hand and said:

Eva Perón rose from a life of poverty to become first lady of Argentina.

I shall always do what the people wish, but I tell you ... that I would rather be Evita than the wife of the president, if this Evita could do anything for the pain of my country; and so now I say I would rather be Evita.

From her words, it seemed Eva did not want to be vice president.

The crowd shouted "No, no." They wanted her to announce that she would run for office. No woman in Argentina had ever held such a high office. As darkness came, many people in the crowd lit the night with torches made out of rolled-up newspapers. They settled down to wait for Eva Perón to speak again. They hoped she would give them a clear answer.

In the years before the Peróns rose to power, corrupt governments denied the Argentine people their political rights. Elections were neither fair nor honest. In addition, there was great poverty throughout the country. Although Argentina was a wealthy country with a strong agricultural industry, most of the wealth remained with a few privileged landowners. The majority worked long days for low wages. They felt hopeless about their future.

Eva Perón had risen from this sort of poverty to become one of the most famous women in the world. Improving conditions for Argentina's poor became her life's goal. She helped provide them with better health care and housing, and she and Juan formed labor unions to fight for better wages and benefits for workers. Poor people and workers of Argentina adored Juan and Eva Perón.

At the same time, many upper-class people disapproved of Eva. They thought of her as low class, hard-hearted, and selfish. Spreading rumors about her past life, they said that she and Juan stole money from the government. Some army officers thought that Eva had too much influence over her husband and in the government. The last thing they wanted was for Eva to become vice president of Argentina. If Juan Perón should die, Argentina would be ruled by a woman.

Eva Perón at work in her office.

The workers, however, saw Eva as their leader, and they wanted her for their vice president. The huge crowd on that August night kept calling for Evita, but she would not say that she would run. She told the people:

*Comrades, it's said throughout the world
that I am a selfish and ambitious woman;
you know very well that this isn't the case.
But you also know that everything I did, it
was never so that I could have any political position in my country.*

The crowd cheered and chanted even louder. Juan Perón was surprised. It seemed that she was more popular than he was!

Finally, Eva said, "Comrades, as General Perón has said, I will do what the people say." When Eva was finished speaking, the crowd went away, but no one was sure if Eva was going to run or not.

In the end, Eva Perón never ran for vice president.

*Eva used her
signature,
broad ges-
tures as she
addressed
the crowd on
August 22, 1951.*

Right after that torch-lit night, she fell ill with cancer. She died in 1952 at the age of 33. After her death, however, stories about her took on new life.

Much of Eva Perón's life was mysterious. In an attempt to keep people from learning about her past, she would not talk about her childhood. She even lied about her age and where she was born. Because they had no facts, both Eva's enemies and friends made up stories about her.

Today, people in Argentina call the stories the Black Myth and the White Myth. According to the Black Myth, Eva Perón was a ruthless woman who used Juan Perón to acquire riches and power. She was cruel to people that she did not like and forced merchants and shopkeepers to give her money.

However, according to the White Myth, Evita was a saint who sacrificed her life to help the poor of Argentina, especially poor women and children. She was devoted to fairness and justice, working tirelessly for the rights of ordinary working people.

Neither the Black Myth nor the White Myth is entirely true. Parts of each myth, however, make up Eva Perón's story. Her work helped improve the lives of the poor and humble, but her efforts were not selfless. By reaching out to the workers, she built political support for her husband and helped keep him in power. In her brief life, Eva Perón was an important, influential person in the history of her country. ✑

2 LIFE ON THE PAMPA

❧

Eva Perón did not always know a life of power and privilege. Maria Eva Duarte was born to middle-class parents in the tiny town of Los Toldos, about 125 miles (200 kilometers) from Argentina's capital, Buenos Aires. All records of her birth were mysteriously destroyed in the 1940s when she met Juan Perón. Historians, however, believe that she was born on May 7, 1919.

Eva's father, Juan Duarte, managed a large farm for wealthy landowners. The farm was located on the pampa, one of the world's best farming and ranching areas. Lying in the center of Argentina, the pampa covers about one-fifth of the country. Farmers grow wheat, corn, alfalfa, and other crops in the fertile soil of the eastern pampa. Huge herds of beef cattle

An Argentine gaucho, or cowboy, watches over a herd of cattle on the pampa in the 1930s.

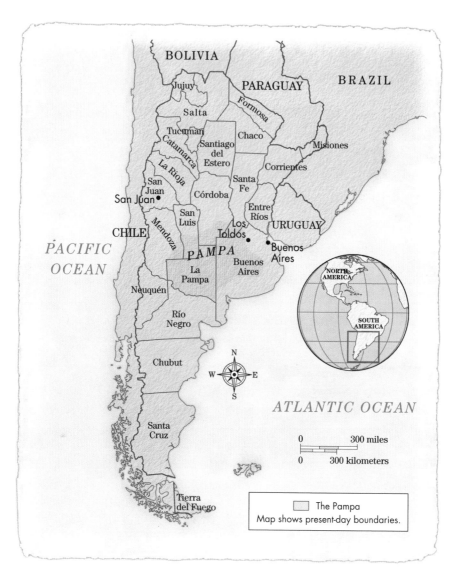

The Pampa
Map shows present-day boundaries.

Argentina is divided into 24 provinces.

graze on pampa grasses in rural parts of the province of Buenos Aires. Gauchos, South American cowboys, look after the big herds.

A network of railroads ran through the pampa,

many of them built and owned by British companies. Trains carried cattle and produce to the city of Buenos Aires, and small towns grew up around railroad stops along the way. Los Toldos was one of those towns.

Eva's father's farm was very successful, and he was paid with a share of the profits. The landowners also gave Duarte some land of his own. Most people living on the pampa did not own land, since just a few wealthy families kept most of it for themselves. Eva's father also owned a car and a house on the main street in Los Toldos. He was friendly and liked to entertain neighbors in his house. He served as the town's justice of the peace, a type of judge who helped settle minor arguments among the town's people. Duarte was an important and popular person in the area.

Argentina is the second-largest country in South America. It lies south of Brazil, South America's largest country, and extends southward toward Antarctica. The Atlantic Ocean borders Argentina on the east. The Andes mountains in the west form the border between Argentina and Chile. Argentina is divided into separate provinces each with their own provincial governments.

Eva's mother was Juana Ibarguren. Eva was the youngest of five children. She had three older sisters—Blanca, Elisa, and Erminda—and a brother, Juan. Duarte never married Eva's mother.

From the time she was born, Eva's life was affected by the politics of Argentina. Her father was

A photograph from the early 1900s shows the building where the Argentine Congress meets. The building is called Congreso Nacional.

successful partly because the people he worked for were extremely powerful. The great landowners of the pampa were in control of Argentina's government, and they voted in representatives who would work for them. They ensured their representatives' position through election fraud, threatening voters with violence or buying their votes. Finally, in 1910, Argentina's Congress passed laws that called for secret ballots and other measures to guarantee honest elections.

In 1919, these laws helped the Radical Party gain power in Buenos Aires Province, where Los Toldos was located. The Radical Party was made up of middle-class citizens. This meant that Argentina was now no longer controlled by a wealthy few.

With the change in power, life became more difficult for Juan Duarte. His wealthy landowner friends had lost much of their political control and influence. Business was not good either, and profits from the farm decreased. Duarte took a different job managing another farm in a nearby area, but it did not work out.

No one is sure why, but Juan Duarte made a decision that would change his family's life. In 1920, when Eva was less than a year old, Duarte left Juana Ibarguren and their five children—his "second family"—and returned to his hometown of Chivilcoy. There he had a wife and several other children. When he lived with Eva's mother, he had supported both families. But when he returned to his "first family," he left Eva's mother with no money. ❧

3 POOR BUT DETERMINED

ⓔⓖⓧⓔⓞ

Juana's family suddenly found itself poor and unpopular. Townspeople looked down on Eva and her brother and sisters. They were children of parents who never married. When Juan Duarte lived with them, life was prosperous. There was plenty of food, nice clothing, a comfortable house, and even a maid. They could no longer afford to live in their nice house on the main street. They moved to a tiny two-room house on a dusty street near the railroad tracks. People gossiped about them, and parents refused to allow their children to play with Eva or her siblings.

Eva's mother, Juana, had to find work to support the family. She owned a sewing machine and decided to earn money by sewing clothes for the townspeople. She worked day and night at her sewing machine.

Towns were few and far between the railroad lines on the great pampa. The towns that emerged were little more than railroad stops.

21 ᐤᐤ

Sores called ulcers developed on her legs. A doctor told her to rest. "I don't have the time," she replied. "If I rest, how shall I work and how will they live?"

With their mother busy at her sewing machine, the children were left to entertain themselves. There was not much for them to do in Los Toldos. The town had a plaza, or central square, with a church and a few stores. Other than the plaza, the town consisted of about four blocks of small houses. At the edge of town, the flat pampa stretched out in all directions. On Saturdays, the children might visit the town's stores, and on Sundays, they attended Mass at the Catholic church.

Eva was a thin little girl with black hair and big brown eyes. Her family called her *la flaca*, which means "skinny" in Spanish. When she was 8 years old, she put on the white smock worn by Argentine schoolgirls and began first grade in Los Toldos. A teacher recalled that Eva was a beautiful girl who seemed to be "a self-absorbed child with an intense inner life, great sensitivity, and great vulnerability."

Eva loved to play with her sister Erminda and their dog, Leon, out by the railroad track. The girls made costumes and played make-believe games. Their big brother, Juan, made kites and other toys for them to play with. All the while, they heard the sound of the sewing machine in the house as their mother worked away. Neither Eva nor her brother or sisters

ever forgot that sound.

In 1926, Eva's father was killed in a car crash. Juana took the whole family to Chivilcoy for the funeral. Duarte's wife did not want his "second family" there, but his brother finally said they could follow the procession to the cemetery if they stayed at the back of the line. The trip to Chivilcoy was the first time Eva had been out of Los Toldos.

In 1930, Eva's oldest sister, Elisa, lost her job at

the post office in Los Toldos. She soon found work at a post office in Junin, a town about 20 miles (32 km) away. Although Junin was a small town, it was bigger than Los Toldos. Juana thought the family would have more opportunities there, so they all moved to Junin.

Eva's sister Blanca became a schoolteacher, and Juan worked as a traveling salesman for the Radical Soap Company. Erminda began high school, and Eva began third grade. With three of her children earning money, Juana was able to quit sewing. She earned a small income by serving lunch to three bachelors who preferred the homemade cooking over anything else in town. Two of these men later married Elisa and Blanca. Life became better for the family.

Eva was inspired by the American star Norma Shearer.

Eva discovered a wonderful new world in Junin—the world of American and European motion pictures. With two theaters in town, Eva went to movies as often as she could. There she lost herself in a fantasy world that was much different from her small town life on the pampa. The movies showed her a world of wealth, big cities, power, and romance.

She loved American movie stars—especially Norma Shearer, one of the biggest movie stars of the 1930s, who, like Eva, came from a poor family.

As Eva grew older, her love for the movies also grew. She collected pictures of movie stars any way she could. She even took Erminda's turn at washing dishes in exchange for photographs from her sister's collection. Eva and her best friend, Elsa, bought the Argentine movie magazine *Sintonía*, from which they cut out pictures of stars and traded them with each other.

Elsa was one of the few girls at school who spoke to Eva. Elsa was an orphan and lived with her two aunts, who liked Eva. Most girls, however, were warned by their mothers to stay away from Eva. Just as in Los Toldos, mothers in Junin did not think that Juana was a respectable woman. This treatment must have hurt Eva very much. She did not believe that her family was treated fairly. In her autobiography, Eva wrote:

> *As far as I can remember, the existence of injustice has hurt my soul as if a nail was being driven into it. From every period of my life, I retain the memory of some injustice tormenting me and tearing me apart.*

During this time, Eva made a plan. She would

The place of Eva's dreams, Buenos Aires, was a bustling city in the 1930s.

escape Junin, the gossips, and her life of poverty by moving to Buenos Aires, becoming a great actress, and finding fame. At first, Eva's family thought this was just a schoolgirl's fantasy. Many girls like Eva dreamed of becoming actresses to break free from the boredom and poverty of life in a pampa town. But by the time Eva was 15, they knew she was quite serious about this plan.

Eva had acted in a school play, and she discovered she had a gift for reciting poetry. The owner of a record shop in Junin set up loudspeakers and a microphone outside his store and encouraged the town's young people to perform in front of the shop on Saturdays. One Saturday, 15-year-old Eva took the microphone and recited a number of poems. This was her first "public broadcast." "Even as a little girl I wanted to recite," she later wrote in her autobiography. "It was as though I wished to say something to others, something important which I felt in my deepest heart."

Shortly after her public recital, Eva told her mother that she was leaving for Buenos Aires to become an actress. Juana was furious. She wanted the family to stay together in Junin. She wanted Eva to find a job or go to school to become a teacher as Blanca had. Then she wanted Eva to marry and settle down. Determined to have a career as an actress, Eva stubbornly refused to even consider taking this path. She and her mother had many arguments. Blanca recalled that Eva showed "the same iron will and determination that would mark her for the rest of her life." Later that year, Eva grabbed onto her chance to go to Buenos Aires. ᘓ

Chapter

4 EVA THE ACTRESS

⤛⤜

There are two stories about how Eva came to live in Buenos Aires. No one knows which is true.

According to one story, Eva fled Junin with a famous tango singer named Agustin Magaldi. She had gone to the Crystal Palace Theater to watch Magaldi perform. Like all tango singers, he sang sad songs with a pained expression on his face. As she watched him onstage, she fell in love with him. After the performance, she begged him to take her to Buenos Aires, and he did.

According to the other story, Eva's mother, Juana, took her to Buenos Aires in 1935. Eva wanted to perform in a talent show and audition at radio stations. At first, Juana refused. But the principal of the school where Blanca had studied to be a teacher

A promotional photo of Eva when she was an actress

convinced her to let Eva try. He told Juana that parents should not stand in the way of their children. Because Juana respected the principal's opinion, she decided to listen to his advice.

Eva and her mother boarded a train for Buenos Aires. Together they went from one radio station to another. At each station, Eva recited poems. Finally, they came to a station that was looking for a young girl to play a role in a radio program. They gave Eva a contract for the job. Juana had no choice but to leave Eva in Buenos Aires with family friends. She had not planned for Eva to actually find a job in radio, and she returned to Junin angry about the situation.

No matter which story is true, Eva now called Buenos Aires home. She returned to Junin for brief visits only.

In 1935, Buenos Aires—the nation's capital—was a thriving city filled with rich and powerful people. Eva could walk in the parklike Plaza de Mayo and see the Casa Rosada at one end. The Casa Rosada, or Pink House, was the government building where the president of Argentina had his offices. Eva walked through neighborhoods where wealthy landowners had built mansions that looked like European palaces. Most of the money in Argentina belonged to families who lived in these houses but spent much of their time in Europe.

But Buenos Aires was also home to under-privileged people. Eva saw the city slums that housed the poor. Times were hard for these people, and many of them did not have jobs or enough food to eat.

By 1935, the Radical Party had fallen out of power, and a coalition of conservative parties called the Concordancia was in control. The Concordancia included land-owners and political groups who condemned the way the Radical Party ran Argentina.

Casa Rosada was originally painted pink in the 1800s to ease tensions between opposing political groups, one whose color was red and one whose color was white.

This coalition got rid of reformers in the civil service and workers' unions, replacing them with their relatives and friends. Anyone who objected was sent to prisons in the coldest regions of southern Argentina. These changes left the workers feeling powerless. All the power lay with the wealthy landowners, who hated and feared the workers. The working and middle classes called the wealthy landowners the oligarchy, which is a government ruled by a few.

Even though Eva was very poor, she was not concerned with the politics of the day. She began her life in Buenos Aires with little money and few clothes or other possessions. Her formal schooling ended after sixth grade, and she had no training as an actress. But what she lacked in education she made up for in determination.

Her job at the radio station did not last long, so Eva found small parts in plays. In 1936, she went on tour with a company that put on performances in small towns across Argentina. She also had roles in radio soap operas and small parts in movies.

The life of an actress in Argentina in the 1930s

Members of the military led the government that took over Argentina in 1930.

was a hard one. Landowners and middle-class people looked down on the profession. Actresses earned little money, bought their own costumes, and paid for lodging when they traveled. Eva lived in tiny rooms in boardinghouses on the road and in Buenos Aires. Though she earned little money, she sent what she could back to her family in Junín.

Meanwhile, radio broadcasting was becoming big business in Argentina. By 1939, Argentina's network of radio broadcasting stations was the second largest in the world. Eva focused her career on radio. That year, she and a partner owned a company that put on radio soap operas and produced a series called *The Biographies of Illustrious Women.*

Radio programs were as important to people in the 1930s and 1940s as television programs are today. People in Buenos Aires and small towns all over Argentina gathered around the radio to hear their favorite programs. They listened to the story unfold through the dialogue of actors and actresses and the sound effects of horses' hooves and slamming doors. The performers stood around microphones in the radio studio and read the script. These actors and actresses became big stars, and magazines featured them in pictures and stories. Eva's picture often appeared in magazines, including *Sintonía*, the same magazine from which she and Elsa once cut photographs of stars. Now little girls in small Argentine towns could cut out pictures of Eva.

Eva's brother, Juan, helped with her radio career by getting the makers of Radical Soap to sponsor her shows. As a result, Eva no longer had to work at convincing radio stations to hire her. Stations wanted Radical Soap to buy advertising time with them, so they were eager to put Eva's shows on the air in an effort to help build good relations with the sponsor. Eva moved her programs to bigger radio stations and earned more money.

By 1943, Eva was a rich and successful star living in a nice apartment in the best neighborhood of

Buenos Aires. In an interview, she said she had:

> ... *reached the height of my career, a very rewarding career which began modestly but grew as I dedicated myself to my work, as I strove to perfect myself and to [take in] the very valuable lessons I received.*

Little did she know that her greatest role in life was soon to begin. ℰ

5 A MARVELOUS DAY

೧᎒᎒᎒᎒᎒᎒᎒᎒᎒

On January 15, 1944, a few dishes rattled on kitchen shelves in Buenos Aires. However, just over 600 miles (960 km) to the west, roofs and walls of houses in the Andes mountains collapsed. A powerful earthquake nearly destroyed the city of San Juan. Thousands of people were buried under bricks, boards, and mud. Rescue workers dug through the rubble, trying to find survivors. Between 6,000 and 7,000 people were killed and about 12,000 others injured. Thousands of people were left homeless.

In Buenos Aires, a 48-year-old army colonel named Juan Domingo Perón decided that he must help the people of San Juan. Perón was the head of the nation's labor department, the Secretariat of Labor and Social Welfare. He organized a benefit to

Colonel Juan Perón in front of a portrait of Jose de San Martin, who helped liberate Argentina from Spanish control in 1816

aid victims of the earthquake and he asked the big stars of Argentina's entertainment world, including Eva, to help. The stars and army officers went through the streets collecting money for the victims.

The benefit ended on January 22 with a night of performances and dancing in a stadium. Since

After the 1944 earthquake, all that remained of many of San Juan's buildings was a pile of rubble.

January is in the middle of summer in Argentina, the weather was warm. Wearing a black dress, long gloves, and a white hat with feathers, Eva arrived at the stadium with an actress friend.

There she saw Juan Perón—a tall, muscular man in a white military uniform with a broad face and a big smile. Perón's wife had died of cancer in 1938, and he had not remarried. Perón was friendly and talked with many of the stars, but he especially liked Eva. They quickly fell in love, and from that day on, Eva's story in many ways became Juan Perón's story. They changed each other's lives and the course of Argentina's history. Eva called January 22, 1944, her "marvelous day."

Juan Perón was born in Lobos, Argentina, on October 8, 1895. Like Eva, his parents were not married when he was born, although they later became husband and wife. Perón grew up on his father's farm in Patagonia, a region in southern Argentina. When he was 16 years old, he went off to military school, then joined the army in 1915. The army sent him to remote posts, where he saw people living in terrible poverty. Sometimes workers went on strike, and the army was called in to break up the strike. Perón felt sorry for the workers, and once he commanded a company of soldiers to give food and water to starving strikers. In 1926, Perón was promoted to captain and sent to Buenos Aires. By the time the army took over the government in 1930, he was a colonel.

In 1943, the military once again took control of Argentina, overthrowing the conservative president who was in power. Perón quickly became known as a key leader in Argentina's military-led government. This government was of concern to leaders in the United States and other countries who feared that Argentina was fascist, or controlled by a dictator with right-wing, authoritarian views. At the time, World War II was raging. The United States, Great Britain, and their allies were at war with two other fascist countries: Germany, under Nazi leader Adolf Hitler, and Italy, under dictator Benito Mussolini. The Allies feared that Argentina might side with

Colonel Peron (third from left) stands with other members of the military-led government in 1944

Germany and Italy, but Argentina remained neutral and did not take sides.

Nonetheless, Perón admired Mussolini. He had visited Italy in the late 1930s and liked the patriotic parades and ceremonies of Mussolini's fascist government. He thought that fascist governments were well run. Perón disliked the British because of their close ties to Argentina's wealthy oligarchy. He did not like that Argentina's railroads and Buenos Aires' buses were British owned.

Benito Mussolini (1883–1945)

As head of the Secretariat of Labor and Social Welfare, Perón made a clever move. He encouraged workers to form unions, with each trade having its own union. A few unions already existed in Argentina, but they were small and mostly powerless. Under Perón, unions had a great deal of freedom. Workers could go on strike to get better pay and benefits. Perón was the first government leader to pay attention to the working class. They became loyal to him because he helped improve their lives. The workers were ready to have power in their country's politics and to follow a strong leader.

From the day they met, Juan and Eva were always together. Eva kept her job at the radio station, and she used the fact that she was Perón's friend to get ahead in her career. She got the radio station to pay her more money, and she was offered her first starring role in a movie. For the movie, she bleached her naturally dark hair. She kept her hair blonde for the rest of her life.

In May 1944, actors and actresses formed a union and elected Eva as their president. Eva then began using her acting talent and position with the radio station to help Perón. Every night, she broadcast

Eva during a radio broadcast in the summer of 1944

programs that supported Perón. Her shows were propaganda, which is an organized effort to spread a particular belief. On these programs, she played a role that was simply called The Woman.

An announcer began each program by saying:

> *Here in the confusion of the streets, where a new sense of purpose is coming to be born ... here among the ... mass of working, suffering, thinking, silent people ... here she is, The Woman.*

Eva then talked about the wonderful changes the government had made for poor working people. She called the changes a revolution. Her program had radio skits about rich women being mad at their maids for unfair reasons. Other skits told about sick and hungry poor people in the countryside. Listeners all over Argentina heard Eva in the role of The Woman talk about how wonderful Perón was and how he was making life better for the workers. They heard her say:

> *The revolution ... came because something painful and hard had grown in the country, deep down, where there is hate and passion and the sense of injustice. ... The revolution was made for exploited workers. ... There was a man who could bring dignity to the notion of work. ... It was he who decisively helped the people's revolution.*

Poor people in the rural areas and workers in the city were becoming loyal to Perón. But wealthy landowners did not like him, and some army officers feared and distrusted him. They thought he had too much power in the government. By 1945, Perón had become minister of war and vice president of Argentina. Eva attended most of Perón's political meetings at his apartment and joined him at union meetings, banquets, and ceremonies. Some of his political friends feared that Eva had too much influence over Juan Perón. Enemies began gossiping about her. Who was she and where did she come from? Eva said nothing about her past, and then people gossiped even more.

In 1945, the military-led government of Argentina became unpopular. The Communist Party, the Radical Party, and conservatives were rival political groups in the country, but they were all united against Perón. They said he was a Nazi, like Hitler. Perón fought back, gathering huge crowds of workers to support him. He spoke against his critics, saying they were controlled by foreigners and corrupt politicians. The country seemed to be divided into two groups—those who were for Perón and those who were against him.

On October 8, 1945, a series of events began that would change Argentina and the course of Eva's life. A group of army officers asked Perón to resign.

A crowd of middle-class men gathered in opposition to Juan Perón in the fall of 1945.

If he did not, the army would once again overthrow government leaders and seize power. The next day, Perón resigned from the government and army. He was depressed. He thought that he and Eva might go away and live a quiet life together. However, a group of army officers arrested Perón and took him to an island in the bay off the coast of Buenos Aries. The public did not know what had happened to him or if he was even still alive. It seemed that the career of Juan Perón was over, and no one seemed to care what would happen to Eva. ❧

6 A Day of Revolution

Chapter

ecↄ∞

Eva promptly asked a judge to have Juan Perón released, but the judge refused. So Perón wrote a letter to the president of Argentina demanding to be released. A friend sent a copy of the letter to newspapers and soon workers across the country were asking what had happened to Perón. Many workers were afraid of what would happen to them if Perón were exiled or killed. They feared that they would lose the gains they had made when Perón was head of the Secretariat of Labor and Social Welfare. The president denied that Perón had been arrested, but the workers did not believe him.

Concerned about Perón and their own fate, the workers decided to take matters into their own hands. Union leaders saw they could work with and through Perón to improve conditions for the workers. Working as a partner with Perón, they called for Argentina's trade union members to go on strike on October 18. The strike was to last for 24 hours.

Just as the sun was rising on October 17—the morning before the general strike was to take place—something strange began to happen outside shops and factories all over Buenos Aires. Groups of workers did not go to their jobs. Led by union officials, they went to the center of the city to find out what had happened to Perón. More and more workers joined in, until a mass of people filled the

A crowd of supporters waved posters of Perón as they asked for the return of their leader.

avenues. They chanted "Perón" as they marched. Their destination was the Plaza de Mayo and the main government building Casa Rosada. By nightfall, an estimated 200,000 people filled the plaza. But Eva was not part of this huge demonstration because she stayed at home as Perón had asked her to do.

The workers had become a powerful political force. They had shut down the city. Neither businesses nor government could operate. The workers demanded their leader, and the government had no choice but to set Perón free.

Just after 11 P.M., spotlights lit up the front of the Casa Rosada, and Perón stepped out on a balcony. The crowd went wild. People cheered and waved torches made of rolled-up newspapers. They chanted his name over and over again. Finally, Perón spoke into a microphone. He told the workers he had retired from the army and he wanted to serve the Argentines. "I want to mix with this sweating mass as a simple citizen," he said.

Then he told them to go home and take the next day off to celebrate their victory in having him freed. For many years, the Revolution of October 17 was celebrated as a national holiday in Argentina, just as

Evita made many of her rousing speeches from the balcony of the Casa Rosada. It was originally built by early Spanish settlers in the 1580s. Workers later added to the building, and it became the office of the president of Argentina.

the Fourth of July is celebrated in the United States.

Juan and Eva did not run away to live a quiet life as Juan had thought, but they did get married. They wed in a civil ceremony in October 1945. Two months later, they had a religious ceremony at a Catholic church in the nearby town of La Plata.

With Eva by his side, Perón declared that he would run for president in the election scheduled for February 24, 1946. Eva was no longer an actress. She was the wife of a presidential candidate. She quit acting and turned her attention to Peron's campaign.

Juan and Eva Perón at a party on the campaign trail.

Newspapers wanted to know more about Eva Perón. Everyone in Argentina knew that Eva had been a famous radio actress, but she would not talk about her past. She did not want anyone to know where or when she had been born, and she would not talk about her life of poverty. Her secrecy added to what became the Black Myth and the White Myth.

Most candidates for president in any country have a political party, but Juan Perón did not. He led a coalition, or group of political parties, of workers and union leaders. Juan and Eva Perón called their supporters the *descomisados*, which in Spanish means "shirtless ones." This term meant that instead of wearing suits and ties as wealthy landowners and middle-class people did, they wore shirts with sleeves rolled up. Rolled-up shirtsleeves became a symbol for Juan and Eva Perón.

The presidential campaign was nasty. Perón's opponents said he was a Nazi and spread rumors about Eva. In turn, Perón said his opponents were supported

The descomisados were working people in Argentina. Eva was always telling the descomisados how much she and Juan Perón loved them. In return, they often showed their love for the Peróns by staging huge demonstrations. For example, workers in a truck driver's union might drive their trucks into downtown Buenos Aires, honk their horns, and tie up traffic to show their affection. Men and women workers marched in big parades to show support for the Peróns.

by Great Britain, the United States, and the oligarchy—all of which were unpopular with the people. There was violence on both sides. When the votes were counted, however, Perón and his supporters running for Congress had won the election.

Argentina ushered in a new type of government when Juan Perón was sworn into office in 1946.

On June 5, 1946, Juan Perón was sworn in as president of Argentina. Juan and Eva Perón moved from a simple apartment in Buenos Aires into the Presidential Palace, a mansion with 283 rooms. The palace was in a suburb of Buenos Aires called Palermo. The community had long been seen as a center of social, cultural and political power because many of the pampa's wealthy landowners owned mansions there. In Palermo, the Peróns stood out as a symbol of a new empowered leadership living among the fading power of the privileged families. Eva Perón now lived in the same neighborhood as her enemies, the oligarchy. She was now the wife of the president of Argentina. ♒

7 ARGENTINA'S FIRST LADY

Chapter

⟵❧⟶

When Eva Perón became the first lady, Argentina was one of the richest countries in the world. Many of the world's countries were in debt because of the fighting and destruction of World War II. By the time the war ended in 1945, bombs had seriously damaged many European cities including London, England, and Berlin and Dresden, Germany. In addition, the United States had dropped atomic bombs on Japan.

To pay for the war, some countries borrowed money from Argentina, and they had to pay it back with interest. Many countries also had to buy wheat and beef from Argentina to feed their people. These loans and food exports made Argentina rich.

Perón saw agricultural industry workers as an area where he could build more political support.

He created costly labor regulations meant to benefit the workers with better wages and work conditions. But these regulations made the production of certain grains more expensive for those in charge. Many landowners quit raising grains that required a lot of attention from workers and switched to crops like oats, which required little man power.

In addition, Perón's government found ways to take part of the profits that farmers and ranchers earned on the products they had exported, angering the farmers and ranchers. To get back at Perón, they began to cut their grain and cattle production. Exports began to drop, and one day this would lead to trouble for Perón.

President Perón (second from left) with a number of key political and economic figures

Meanwhile, Perón used the money to establish what he called a New Argentina. He improved Argentina's industries. He nationalized the railroads, putting them under the government's control. He told the workers they could form even more unions. Perón called himself a worker, and he promised to work harder than any president had ever worked.

Juan was a smart and ambitious man. He did not help workers simply out of concern for the people. He helped them in order to gain their support. As long as the workers voted for Perón, he could stay in power.

Eva also went to work in this New Argentina. She went to factories to visit with workers, and she learned what was important to union leaders. An assistant went to union meetings with Eva to take notes and give the first lady suggestions. At first, Eva Perón was shy, but she soon learned to use her acting abilities to make dramatic speeches in support of her husband. She pointed her finger in the air or gestured with her hands. Her eyes looked out on the people with great passion. "Perón is everything," she said. "He is the soul, the nerve,

When Juan and Eva Perón came to power in 1946, about 500,000 workers belonged to unions. By 1950, the number of workers in unions had grown to more than 2 million. All the unions of Argentina belonged to one big organization called the General Confederation of Labor (CGT), which Perón controlled.

the hope and the reality of the Argentine people." Eva was Perón's greatest supporter, and she could say things that he could not.

Eva started working three days a week in a small government office. Before long, she had a group of offices in the Ministry of Labor. Every morning, Eva went to work in the chauffeur-driven presidential limousine.

I could have been a president's wife in the same way that others were. It is a simple and agreeable role: appear on holidays, receive honors, 'dress up' and follow protocol. ... But I was not just the spouse of the president of the republic, I was also the wife of the leader of the Argentine people.

Juan had a double identity as president of Argentina and as leader of the working people. Eva said:

I would need to have one also: I am Eva Perón, the wife of the president ... and I am also Evita, the wife of the leader of a people who have deposited in him all their faith, hope, and love.

In the role of Eva Perón, she did the official things that a president's wife was expected to do. But in the role of Evita, she became Perón's direct contact with the descomisados. She saw herself as a bridge between Perón and the shirtless ones.

Union members came to Evita's office to ask for help. She used all the power of the presidency to cut through red tape and get things done. For example, a mother might tell Evita about her sick child in a town where there was no hospital. Evita would see that

Argentina's poor came to Eva's office to personally ask for her help.

the child received medical care. Evita might be told of women living in shacks, and she would get them into decent houses.

Eva had many critics. Some politicians and army officers said that she meddled in government affairs. The high society members of the oligarchy saw her as a lower-class woman who did not know her place. Few newspapers supported the Peróns, so to get good publicity, Eva bought a newspaper named *Democracia* in early 1947. The editors understood that they should fill the paper with pictures of Eva.

Eva used Juan's power to get money. The government controlled the Central Bank, so when Eva decided to buy Democracia, she went to Central Bank to ask for a loan. The bank, of course, loaned her the money to purchase the newspaper.

When Eva bought *Democracia*, the paper printed about 6,000 copies of each issue. However, after the newspaper began printing pictures of Eva, circulation grew enormously. Photographers took pictures of Eva in magnificent gowns at official events in the Colon Theater, a beautiful opera house. When pictures of a big gala ran in *Democracia*, the editors printed 400,000 copies. The newspaper gave Eva favorable publicity, and her elegant image helped the newspaper sell more copies.

In June 1947, Eva visited Europe. Spain's ruler, a dictator named Francisco Franco, had officially invited her to visit Spain. Argentina was the only nation that would deal with Spain's fascist government. After the war, the people in Spain were very poor and hungry, and Argentina lent Spain money

Eva visited several major cities during her 1947 tour.

to buy wheat. Juan could not visit Spain himself because he did not want the United States and other democracies to think that he, too, was a fascist. Eva could go, however.

In addition to Spain, she was to visit Italy, France, and Portugal, then stop at Uruguay and Brazil on the way home. The Argentine government said that the purpose of her trip was to stretch "a rainbow of beauty" between the New World and the Old World. Her European trip was nicknamed the "Rainbow Tour."

At a farewell reception the night before she left, she said, "I am going as the representative of the working people, of my dear descomisados. I leave my heart behind with them." A huge crowd turned out at the airport to see her off. It was Eva's first trip to Europe and her first ride on an airplane.

When Eva's plane landed in Madrid, the capital of Spain, an astonishing 3 million people waited to greet her. They ran beside her car as it traveled through the streets of Madrid. Not many foreign figures visited Spain in the 1940s, and the people were excited to see someone so important. In addition, the Spanish people were grateful for the food they received from Argentina. They wanted to show Eva Perón their love and thanks. Although the people embraced her, Eva was afraid during the nights on

Francisco Franco ruled Spain from 1939 until his death in 1975. Franco rose to power after he led the fascist Nationalist Army in victory over the government's Loyalist forces in a Spanish civil war during the early 1930s. After Franco gained control of Spain, he called himself El Caudillo, which in Spanish means "the leader."

TIME

THE WEEKLY NEWSMAGAZINE

EVA PERÓN
Between two worlds, an Argentine rainbow.

Boris Chaliapin

the entire European trip. She would not sleep alone and insisted that her traveling companion stay with her. Eva never said what she feared exactly.

Eva Perón toured Spain for 15 days. She attended banquets, plays, folk dance performances, and even a bullfight. Franco awarded her Spain's highest honor, the Grand Cross of Isabella the Catholic. The visit to Spain made Eva Perón famous throughout Europe. People in other countries wanted to meet this renowned woman.

In Italy, she had a private meeting with Pope Pius XII. She then visited Portugal, France, and Switzerland before returning home by ship. Thousands of cheering Argentines turned out on the waterfront to greet her. Her European trip lasted three months.

The wealthy women of Argentina's high society disapproved of Eva Perón's trip to Europe. They thought she was trying to fit in with them by imitating their grand tours of Europe. The women of the oligarchy took every opportunity to snub Eva. ❧

8 POWER FROM THE POOR

৵৶৴

Juan Perón's way of ruling became known as Perónism. Patriotism and social justice were important causes for his followers, the Perónists. He raised workers' wages, while his government took control of many of Argentina's industries and invested government money to improve them. Perón wanted to build the economy and industry so Argentina would be a major power in Latin America.

After World War II ended, the United States and the Soviet Union became rivals. The United States was a capitalist democracy. The Soviet Union was a communist dictatorship. The tension between the two nations was called the Cold War. Across the world, support was voiced for one nation or the other, but Perón did not take sides. He believed that

Juan and Eva Perón at an official reception

Argentina should be neutral.

Although Juan Perón was a strong leader on his own, Eva played a major role in helping him stay in power. She could freely praise Perón and Perónism. Her speeches and radio broadcasts were great propaganda, and Eva was always in the news.

Juan and Eva Perón formed a "cult of personality." They used the media, public appearances, and mass demonstrations to encourage support and even love from the working poor. In fiery speeches, Eva spoke about how much Perón loved the working people and how much he had done for them. Perónists did not believe that there should be an upper class, a middle class, and a lower class. They wanted just one class—the working class.

Eva warned constantly about the dangers from the upper class. She warned army officers and union leaders about the dangers falling out of rank and falling in with the enemies of the people and the enemies of Perón. "In our blood," she warned, "we all have the seeds of selfishness that could turn us into enemies of the people and its cause."

Eva also brought a huge group of new voters to

Eva was known for her impassioned speeches.

support Juan Perón—the women of Argentina. Since the early 1900s, there had been growing support for women's suffrage, or right to vote, in Argentina. Despite this effort, only men were allowed to vote.

Eva was the most powerful woman in Argentina, but she couldn't even cast a vote in her husband's election. Eva began to give speeches in favor of votes for women. Juan, too, supported women's suffrage. He made sure that the Perónists in Congress gave Argentine women the right to vote in 1947.

Eva Perón wanted the working women of Argentina to use their votes to support her husband. In 1949, she formed the Perónist Women's Party, At the first gathering of her new women's party, Eva told the Perónist women that they had to fight the discrimination and injustice suffered by working women.

Eva addresses a women's meeting during a five-day Perónist congress.

People who support women's rights are called feminists. Eva Perón offered an unusual kind of feminism. "To be a Perónist is, for a woman, to be loyal and to have blind confidence in Perón," she told the women. Eva called for women to leave their families for a time and set up Perónist Women's Party offices all over the country. She told the women that they must work tirelessly for Perón.

People who did not like Eva accused her of being a fanatic. Although her critics were saying she was overly devoted to Perónism, Eva was honored rather than insulted. She thought that being a fanatic for Perón and the shirtless ones was a wonderful thing to be.

> *Only fanatics do not give up. ... To serve the people, one has to be prepared for any-thing—including death. ... That is why I am a fanatic. I would give my life for Perón and for the people.*

Four million women turned out to vote for the first time in 1951. Most of them voted for Perón and the Perónist Party candidates. Many women ran for office, and voters elected 29 women to Congress. Women also ran for and won offices in provinces and towns all over Argentina.

At first, Juan and Eva Perón did many things to help the poor and make Argentina more democratic.

Yet many of his opponents suspected that Perón was up to no good. "Everything he does is in the name of democracy and social betterment," said one, "yet we sense the smell of evil in the air."

Juan Perón gradually became a dictator. Because of his ambition, power and control became more important to him than fairness and justice. He clamped down on those who criticized him, removing them from jobs or even sending them to jail. He especially did not like to read critical articles and he found ways to silence disapproving newspapers. Government building inspectors fined one newspaper for not having proper fans—until the paper stopped criticizing Perón. Government officials shut down another newspaper, saying the printing presses made too much noise.

Meanwhile, Eva made fiery speeches against Juan's enemies. Her hatred came through in her words. She said that enemies of Juan's were enemies of the working people of Argentina. She wrote:

> *From the first moment [I met Juan] I saw the shadow of his enemies, stalking him like vultures from above or like vicious snakes from the beaten earth.*

Eva saw herself as his vigilant protector. She was also protecting her own power by ensuring Juan remained in power.

Just as she passionately hated Juan's enemies, Eva passionately loved the poor people:

> *It is nice to live with the people. Feeling them close, suffering their pain, and rejoicing in the simple joy of their hearts. ... That is why the people make me happy and give me pain.*

Juan and Eva Perón relied on the descomisados to keep them in power. In turn, the descomisados relied on the Peróns for help and support. ❧

Hasta el último rincón del país

"Prefiero ser solamente EVITA a la esposa del Presidente, si ese EVA es pronunciado para remediar algo en cualquier hogar de mi patria"

**CAMPAÑA
PRO-AYUDA SOCIAL**

MARIA EVA DUARTE DE **PERO**

9

EVITA'S FOUNDATION

✦◦⟨✕⟩◦✦

For many years, the wealthy women of the oligarchy had run a charity called the Beneficent Society. The society set up orphanages and homes for poor senior citizens, and it operated some hospitals. By tradition, the wife of Argentina's president was the honorary president of the society. However, the wealthy women could not imagine having Eva as their honorary president. They sent word that she was "too young." Eva was hurt and angry. She had the government shut down the Beneficent Society. She said that in the New Argentina, charity would no longer be needed because social justice would ensure that all people's needs were met.

When Eva became first lady, needy people started coming to her beautiful government offices to see

---

Eva was featured on a political propaganda postcard for a "Campaign for Social Welfare."

her. She saw people who needed food and clothing. She saw people who needed a decent place to live. She saw mothers with children who were sick and could not afford doctors or medicine. Eva did everything she could to help these people. She remembered what it was like to be poor:

> *The suffering of the poor, the humble, the great pain of so much of humanity without sun and without sky hurts me too much to keep quiet.*

Poor people far away began sending her letters asking for help. By early 1948, she was getting about 12,000 letters a day. Union officials and workers gave her donations of food, clothing, and other things. Evita's work needed more organization. The Eva Perón Foundation was established in July 1948.

The elderly women of the Beneficent Society made orphans wear blue uniforms and shave their heads. At Christmastime, the children had to go door to door collecting money for the Beneficent Society.

Evita did not want the foundation to be like the Beneficent Society or like other welfare organizations she had seen on her trip to Europe. She said that these examples had taught her to stay away from charities "created according to the criteria of the rich. ... [W]hen the rich think about the poor they have poor ideas."

The government, unions, businesses, and ordinary people gave the foundation money for its work with the poor. But their charity was not completely voluntary. Eva quietly suggested that union members would no longer receive raises if they refused to give two days' wages a year to

The volunteer workers of the Institute for Work of Argentina awarded Eva with an insignia.

the foundation. Big business leaders faced jail time and heavy fines if they refused to give. Soon the government passed laws to ensure money kept flowing in.

All this money was never formally counted because Eva claimed "keeping books on charity is capitalistic nonsense. I just use the money for the poor. I can't stop to count it." Because the foundation did not have accounting records, it seemed likely to some people that Eva was keeping some of the money for herself. After all, she kept several bank

Eva dressed in furs and jewels.

accounts and owned an impressive collection of expensive jewelry. The charge, however, was never proven.

Although the source and use of funds were questionable, the Eva Perón Foundation had worthy goals. It would give scholarships to students and tools to workers. It would build schools, hospitals, and houses for poor families. Eva did not see the work of the foundation as charity. She considered her work social aid, which had long-term goals of providing the poor with the things they needed to make permanent improvements, such as education and health care. She felt charity merely provided short-term relief for the poor:

> *Charity humiliates, and social aid dignifies. ... Charity prolongs the situation; social aid solves it. ... Charity is the generosity of the fortunate; social aid remedies social inequalities.*

The Eva Perón Foundation had simple rules. Evita was appointed leader of the foundation for life. All requests went through her. A person in need simply had to write a letter to her, and they would get an appointment to see her. Evita's office rooms and the hallway outside overflowed with more people every day. Union officials and important people gathered in one room. Women and children dressed in rags filled another. The Peróns made sure to capitalize on the favorable image of Eva reaching out to the poor. Newspaper photographers lingered about, and big floodlights lit up the faces of the people who came to see Evita. Her charity work was good publicity for Juan and his Perónist government.

Eva worked very hard. She got up every morning at 5:30 A.M. and had breakfast with Juan. At 8 A.M., she began holding meetings. She and Juan took a long lunch break, then she went back to work. She often worked until midnight. On some evenings, she attended parties with her husband. Even though Eva claimed to be like the working people, she loved to wear beautiful gowns, furs, and expensive jewelry.

In four years, Eva and her foundation built 1,000 schools and more than 60 hospitals. The foundation set up nursing schools that trained about 1,300 nurses every year to serve in clinics in city slums or isolated rural towns. Another foundation project established a clean, safe place for single working women to live in Buenos Aires. There were homes for unwed mothers and the elderly.

She also created a unique children's city with small-scale houses and other buildings to house about 200 children who were orphans or whose parents could not care for them.

Evita believed that schoolchildren and workers needed vacations, so she created resorts where

Children sit outside a small-scale building in Eva's children's city.

they could go free of charge.

Even some of Eva and Juan Perón's political opponents had to admire what she accomplished. One commented:

If we had done for the workers a tiny fraction of what Evita had done there never would have been a Perón and she would still be a bad actress.

Evita began to work harder and harder. She became a fanatic about helping the poor. She worked longer and longer hours. She did not get enough sleep. When asked about her busy schedule, she replied, "All these people you see? I am nothing; my work is everything. Time is my greatest enemy."

Time *was* her greatest enemy. Eva was developing a cancer that would soon claim her life.

Meanwhile, she wanted to run for vice president with Juan Perón in the November 1951 election. All of the unions promised to support her. They organized a huge rally on August 22, 1951, and the people filled the street, begging her to run. The next day, she collapsed from pain caused by her disease. Eva Perón gave a radio speech a few days later, telling Argentines that she would not accept the nomination as vice president.

Every day, Eva became sicker, but she would not let doctors operate. Finally, she agreed. After the surgery, she was very weak, but officials brought

Evita loved to give gifts to the poor. Every Christmas, she saw that everyone got a bottle of cider and some sweets and that children got toys. Local post offices gave out the presents. Each present carried a greeting and a picture of Juan and Eva Perón.

the ballot to her hospital room. She voted for the first—and last—time in a presidential election, which resulted in a huge victory. The last time Eva appeared in public was at Juan Perón's second inauguration as president. She rode with him in an open car in a

Eva had to vote from her hospital bed.

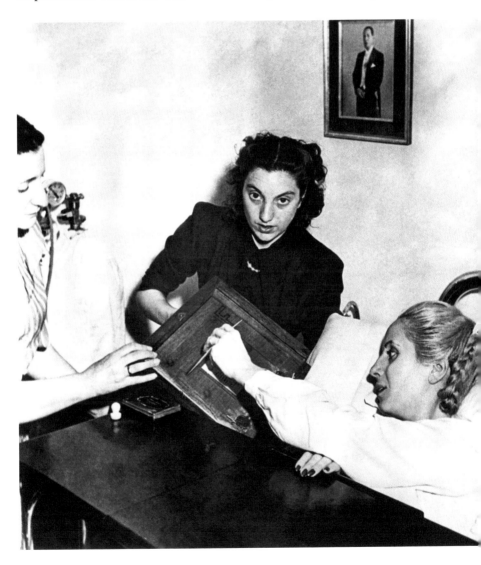

In her last public appearance, Eva rode beside Juan in a procession for his second inauguration.

parade. Eva waved to the cheering crowds. She was so weak that a special brace under her fur coat held her up.

She wrote a final booklet called *My Message*. In it, she said:

> *Sickness and pain have brought me close to God, and I have realized that everything that is happening to me and all that is making me suffer is not unfair. When I married Perón, I had every opportunity to take the wrong path that leads to the [excitement] of high places. Instead, God took me down my people's roads and because I followed them, I have come to receive the affection of men, women, children, and the elderly as no one else has. But I do ask God for a little vacation from my suffering.*

The government told the people of Argentina that Eva Perón was very sick and was probably going to die. Millions of workers went to church and said prayers for her. Members of the Perónist Women's Party knelt on the street outside the presidential residence and sobbed. She grew weaker and lost weight. On July 26, 1952, Eva Perón died. She was 33. ❧

HOMENAJE A EVA PERON

10 THE LEGEND LIVES ON

⟨⟩

Evita became even more famous after she died. The working people of Argentina felt terrible grief when they heard the news broadcast over the radio. Their beloved Evita was gone.

Juan Perón wanted to build a great monument to Evita. He did not want to bury her. He wanted to keep her body looking just as it did when she was alive. He found a doctor who knew how to preserve bodies and made plans to have hers placed in a glass coffin so people could see Eva for years to come. The body of Lenin, the leader of the 1917 Communist Revolution in Russia, had been preserved this way. For most of the 20th century, his body lay in a glass coffin, and millions of people visited Lenin's tomb. Perón wanted Eva to have this kind of tomb. The

In mourning on August 2, 1952, Argentines held up torches and looked to a huge portrait of their late first lady.

doctor began working on Eva's body.

Millions of people poured into Buenos Aires as soon as they heard that Evita had died. They piled huge mounds of flowers around the government building where she had worked. Even though it was cold and raining, crowds filled the streets for 10 blocks around the building. Juan and other government officials knew the funeral would be massive.

Before the preservation process could be finished, Evita's body was taken to the Ministry of Labor where people could pay their last respects. The turnout was huge—officials were unable to count how many millions of people came, but they lined up day and night for two weeks to view the body. At night, they lit torches and burned candles. Finally, Eva Perón's body was taken to the headquarters of Argentina's main labor union. There the doctor continued to work on Eva's body for the next three years.

After Evita's death, Argentines' grief took over and they honored her in unusual ways. A union-controlled newspaper claimed that the face of the moon had become the face of Eva Perón's—when viewed just the right way. The government declared that Argentine men were to wear black ties forever.

Meanwhile, Argentina was facing economic hardship. Business was not very good. The country was feeling the effect of the dwindling wheat and beef export business. Production had

Millions of people came to view Eva Perón's body.

been declining since 1945 and dipped even further in 1951 and 1952 when a drought hit the pampa. Perón's government even had to ban the sale of beef on certain days to ensure supplies within the country didn't run out. Without money from exports, Perón no longer had the funds for workers' raises or other social reforms.

Argentina was no longer one of the richest countries. Inflation, a rise in prices, made everything more expensive. People had a hard time making ends meet. Middle-class people blamed Juan Perón and his economic policies. Fighting broke out with workers on one side and the upper class, middle class, Catholic Church, and many army officers on the other side. In 1955, the army seized power and overthrew the government. Juan Perón was forced into exile in Spain.

In the chaos of the political revolution, Eva Perón's body disappeared. No one knew who had taken it, and no one knew where it was, but the legend of Evita continued to grow. People who loved her told stories that made up the White Myth. They thought that Evita was like the Virgin Mary—pure and holy. The unions even asked the Catholic Church to declare her a saint.

Working people made up stories about how Evita had organized the crowds that freed Juan Perón in October 1945. But these stories were not true: the unions, not Eva, were responsible for the march and demonstration. Working people also told stories about how Evita had helped them or

their friends. They called her the "Lady of Hope" and the "Good Fairy." They saw her as the ideal Argentine woman.

A torch lit parade honored Eva on the first anniversary of her death.

Schoolchildren learned to say a prayer to Eva:

Our little Mother, thou who art in heaven,
Good fairy laughing amongst the angels,
Evita I promise to be as good as you wish
me to be …

People who hated Eva Perón told stories that made up the Black Myth. They said that she used Perón to grab power for herself, and they accused her of using her Rainbow Tour of Europe to deposit money in her secret bank accounts in Switzerland. They said that she threatened to put merchants in Argentina out of business if they did not donate money to the Eva Perón Foundation. Then, they said, she stole money from the foundation to pay for her expensive gowns, furs, and jewelry. They also accused her of sending upper-class people and others she did not like to jail.

They called her "that woman." After Juan Perón went into exile, no one was allowed to speak about the years when Eva and Juan were in power. But working-class people kept asking, "Where is the body of Eva Perón?"

The government that replaced Perón was afraid of Evita's legend. They feared that people would flock to her tomb if they buried her in Argentina. Because they thought that working people might use the symbol of Evita to start another revolution, army officers took her body to Italy and buried it in a grave with someone else's name on it. Still, that did not stop Evita from becoming a powerful symbol.

Conditions in Argentina continued to decline, and a number of Perónists began to rebel against the military-controlled government. The rebels were

Argentina faced much conflict in the years after Eva's death. Police fired tear gas at Peron supporters in 1964.

called guerillas. They made Evita a symbol for this resistance, saying she would have been a guerilla if she were alive. In 1970, hoping to find out where she was buried, a group of guerillas kidnapped the general who was responsible for taking Evita's body.

When the general would not tell where the body was, they killed him. The general, however, left a letter with his lawyer telling where Eva's body was located. After 17 years, the mystery was solved.

In 1973, the military allowed free elections. Juan Perón returned from Spain and again ran for president and won. By this time, he had married his third wife, Isabel Martinez de Perón. Isabel saw to it that Evita's body was returned to Argentina. In 1976, Eva Perón was finally buried in a Duarte family tomb in the Recoleta Cemetery in Buenos Aires.

Today, the memory of Eva Perón is alive and well. In 1978, *Evita*, a musical based on her life, became a huge success. In 1996, *Evita* was made into a motion picture, sparking renewed interest in the

The Recoleta Cemetery is like a miniature city in the most fashionable area of Buenos Aires. Great stone mausoleums (burial places) are lined up in rows like houses on streets. Only the wealthiest Argentines can afford to be buried there. Admirers of Eva Perón, however, managed to erect a black stone mausoleum for the Duarte family. This is where Evita is buried along with her family members. Some people think it is strange that Eva Perón is buried alongside her worst enemies, the oligarchy. There are always flowers laid at the tomb of Evita.

The Duarte family tomb where Eva was finally buried

life of Eva Perón. And in Buenos Aires, Eva's chosen home, the Evita Museum tells the story of her life and of the White and Black Myths. Even today, decades after her death, Eva Perón's legend lives on. ✎

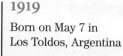

PERÓN'S LIFE

1919

Born on May 7 in
Los Toldos, Argentina

1920

Father leaves Eva's
"second family" in
Los Toldos and returns
to his "first family"

1920

1919

World War I peace
conference begins at
Versailles, France

1920

American women get
the right to vote

League of Women Voters

WORLD EVENTS

1926

Father is killed
in a car accident
on January 8

1930

Moves with family
to Junin

1935

Moves to
Buenos Aires
to become
an actress

1930

1929

The U.S. stock
exchange collapses
and severe worldwide
economic depression
sets in

1933

Nazi leader Adolf Hitler
is named chancellor
of Germany

PERÓN'S LIFE

1944

Meets Colonel Juan Perón in January at a benefit for earthquake victims

1943

Wins fame and wealth as a radio actress

1945

Marries Juan Perón in October

1940

1939

German troops invade Poland; Britain and France declare war on Germany; World War II begins

1945

World War II ends; the United Nations is founded

WORLD EVENTS

1946

Becomes the first lady of Argentina in June following Perón's election as president

1947

Leaves for the Rainbow Tour of Europe on June 6

1946

Nazi war criminals are executed after trials in Nuremberg, Germany

1947

India becomes independent of British rule

PERÓN'S LIFE

1948

Establishes
the Eva Perón
Foundation
in July

1949

Founds the
Perónist Women's
Party and becomes
its president in July

1949

Birth of the
People's Republic
of China

1948

The modern
nation of Israel
is founded

WORLD EVENTS

1951

Diagnosed with cancer; votes for the first and last time from her hospital bed

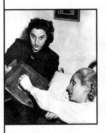

1952

Attends the second inauguration of Juan Perón in June; dies at the age of 33 on July 26

1950

1951

Libya gains its independence with help from the United Nations

1950

North Korea invades South Korea, which begins the Korean War

1952

The Walter-McCarran Act allows Japanese immigrants to become naturalized citizens of the United States

NAME: Maria Eva Duarte Perón

NICKNAME: Evita

DATE OF BIRTH: May 7, 1919

BIRTHPLACE: Los Toldos, Argentina

FATHER: Juan Duarte

MOTHER: Juana Ibarguren

SPOUSE: Juan Perón (1895–1974)

DATE OF MARRIAGE: October 18, 1945

DATE OF DEATH: July 26, 1952

PLACE OF BURIAL: Buenos Aires, Argentina

FURTHER READING

Dechancie, John. *Juan Peron*. New York: Chelsea House, 1998

Fearns, Daisy, and Les Fearns. *Argentina*. Austin, Texas: Raintree, 2004.

Krull, Kathleen, and Kathryn Hewitt (illustrator). *Lives of Extraordinary Women*. San Diego: Raintree, 2000.

Parker, Janice. *Political Leaders*. New York: Crabtree, 1991.

LOOK FOR MORE SIGNATURE LIVES BOOKS ABOUT THIS ERA:

Benazir Bhutto: *Pakistani Prime Minister and Activist*
ISBN 0-7565-1578-5

Fidel Castro: *Leader of Communist Cuba*
ISBN 0-7565-1580-7

Winston Churchill: *British Soldier, Writer, Statesman*
ISBN 0-7565-1582-3

Jane Goodall: *Legendary Primatologist*
ISBN 0-7565-1590-4

Adolf Hitler: *Dictator of Nazi Germany*
ISBN 0-7565-1589-0

Queen Noor: *American-born Queen of Jordan*
ISBN 0-7565-1595-5

Joseph Stalin: *Dictator of the Soviet Union*
ISBN 0-7565-1597-1

On the Web

For more information on *Eva Perón,* use FactHound.

1. Go to *www.facthound.com*
2. Type in a search word related to this book or this book ID: 0756515858
3. Click on the *Fetch It* button.

FactHound will find Web sites related to this book.

Historic Sites

Museo Evita
Lafinur 2988 Palermo
Buenos Aires, Argentina
011-54-11-4807-9433
Located in a building once used for one of Evita's social projects, housing young working women, the museum contains dresses, photos, film, and other items that tell about Eva Perón

Casa Rosada
Hipolito Yrigoyen 211
Plaza de Mayo
Buenos Aires, Argentina
011-54-11-4343-3051
The government office building where Eva Perón made many impassioned speeches

coalition
a union of two or more groups, such as political parties

communist
a supporter of an economic system in which property is owned by the government or community and profits are shared

general strike
a strike to shut down major businesses and industries by workers in unions

nationalized
to take privately owned industries and services and place them under government control

Nazi
a person who supports the policies of Adolf Hitler and his political group, the National Socialist German Workers' Party

oligarchy
a government in which only a few people have power to rule all others

Perónists
people who support policies of Juan Perón and the Perónist Party

protocol
rules of etiquette for government officials

ruthless
without kindness or mercy

sponsor
to finance a program in exchange for advertising

unions
organized groups of workers who try to improve working conditions and pay

Chapter 1

Page 10, line 1: Nicholas Fraser and Marysa Navarro. *Evita: The Real Life of Eva Perón*, New York: W.W. Norton, 1996, p. 144.

Page 12, line 1: Ibid., p. 145.

Page 12, line 10: Ibid., p. 146.

Chapter 3

Page 22, line 2: Ibid., p. 6.

Page 22, line 20: Ibid., p. 8.

Page 25, line 21: Ibid., p. 5.

Page 27, line 9: "To Be Evita, Part I." (Trans. Dolane Larson) Eva Perón Historical Research Foundation. 1997. 11 April 2005. www.evitaperon.org/part1.htm.

Page 27, line 23: Blanca Alvarez. "Our True Life." Evita Perón Historical Research Foundation. 1998-2002. 11 April 2005. www.evitaperon.org/mens.htm.

Chapter 4

Page 35, line 2: "To Be Evita, Part I."

Chapter 5

Page 43, line 6: *Evita: The Real Life of Eva Perón*, p. 42.

Page 43, line 21: Ibid., p. 43.

Chapter 6

Page 49, line 23: Ibid., p. 67.

Chapter 7

Page 57, line 27: Ibid., p. 112.

Page 58, line 12: "To Be Evita, Part II." (Trans. Dolane Larson) Eva Peron Historical Research Foundation. 1997. 11 April 2005. www.evitaperon.org/part2.htm.

Page 58, line 24: Ibid.

Page 63, line 8: *Evita: The Real Life of Eva Perón*, p. 90.

Chapter 8

Page 68, line 25: Eva Peron. *Evita: In My Own Words*. (Trans. Laura Dail). New York: New Press, 1996, p. 56.

Page 71, line 3: *Evita: The Real Life of Eva Perón*, p. 107.

Page 71, line 15: *Evita: In My Own Words*, p. 23.

Page 72, line 2: *Evita: The Real Life of Eva Perón*, p. 102.

Page 73, line 9: *Evita: In My Own Words*, p. 51.

Page 73, line 18: Ibid., p. 73.

Chapter 9

Page 76, line 10: Ibid., p. 49.

Page 76, line 24: *Evita: The Real Life of Eva Perón*, p. 117.

Page 78, line 6: Barnes, John. *Evita, First Lady: A Biography of Eva Perón.* New York: Grove Press, 1978, p. 115.

Page 79, line 6: Ibid., p. 120.

Page 80, line 27: Ibid., p. 160.

Page 82, line 4: *Evita: The Real Life of Eva Perón*, p. 124.

Page 83, line 2: *Evita: In My Own Words*, p. 83.

Alvarez, Blanca. "Our True Life." Evita Perón Historical Research Foundation. 1998-2002. 11 April 2005. www.evitaperon.org/mens.htm.

Barnes, John. *Evita, First Lady: A Biography of Eva Perón.* New York: Grove Press, 1978.

Brown, Jonathan C. *A Brief History of Argentina.* New York: Checkmark Books, 2004.

Evita Perón Historical Research Foundation. 4 November 2005. www.evitaperon.org.

Fraser, Nicholas, and Marysa Navarro. *Evita: The Real Life of Eva Perón.* New York: W. W. Norton, 1996.

Perón, Eva. *Evita: In My Own Words.* (Trans. Laura Dail). New York: New Press, 1996.

Rock, David. *Argentina, 1516-1982: From Spanish Colonization to the Falklands War.* Berkeley: University of California Press, 1985.

Darlene R. Stille is the author of more than 80 books for young people, including collections of biographies. She grew up in Chicago and attended the University of Illinois, where she discovered her love of writing. She now lives and writes in Michigan.

Hulton Archive/Getty Images, cover (top), 4–5, 72; AFP/Getty Images, cover (bottom), 2, 8, 52, 59, 66, 69, 83, 89, 101 (left); Bettmann/Corbis, 11, 28, 35, 38, 45, 48, 81, 84, 86, 91, 101 (right); Keystone/Getty Images, 12, 41, 42, 54, 56, 60, 77, 93, 98 (top left); Mary Evans Picture Library, 14, 33, 96 (top); Hulton-Deutsch Collection/Corbis, 18, 20; Caroline Penn/Corbis, 23; John Kobal Foundation/Getty Images, 24; Topical Press Agency/Getty Images, 26, 97 (top); Sergio Pitamitz/Corbis, 31; Hart Preston/Time Life Pictures/Getty Images, 36; Timepix/Time Life Pictures/Getty Images, 40, 98 (top right); Thomas D. McAvoy/Time Life Pictures/Getty Images, 46, 50, 99; Time Life Pictures/Getty Images, 64; Marie Hansen/Time Life Pictures/Getty Images, 70, 100 (top); Private Collection, Archives Charmet/Bridgeman Art Library, 74; Library of Congress, 78, 96 (bottom), 97 (bottom), 98 (bottom left); Pablo Corral V/Corbis, 95; Corel, 98 (bottom right), 101 (bottom); Brand X Pictures, 100 (bottom).